THIS JOURNAL BELONGS TO

....

MY
Bible Study
JOURNAL

Peace for My Anxious Heart

180 Bible Readings for Women

Donna K. Maltese

BARBOUR
PUBLISHING

INTRODUCTION

When Christ died He left a will in which He gave His soul to His Father,
His body to Joseph of Arimathea, His clothes to the soldiers, and His
mother to John. But to His disciples, who had left all to follow Him, He
left not silver or gold, but something far better—His PEACE!
MATTHEW HENRY, MINISTER AND AUTHOR

Welcome to *My Bible Study Journal: Peace for My Anxious Heart*, a place
where you can connect with God, His Word, and His Spirit. This is your
doorway into a quiet time of prayer, reading, and reflection, a way of dis-
covering what God may be speaking into your life and what He's revealing
to you and you alone so that you will know where to go, what to do, how
to think, what to say.

Within these pages, you'll find five topical Bible reading plans (one
page per day) in the following areas to help you find, cultivate, choose,
keep, and sow God's peace:

Each of the 180 days contains that day's specific aspect of peace, a scripture reading, and two or more journaling prompts.

Before beginning each day's Bible passage, *pray* for the Holy Spirit's
illumination. Make it your intention to *listen* to what God is saying. Then
and only then, *read* and *absorb* the Bible passage for that day. Afterward,
before looking at any commentary or considering that day's journaling
prompts, *mark* the verse or passage that specifically speaks to your heart
and soul in this time and place—whether or not you understand why.
Then go to the journaling prompts. Carefully read each one, then *reflect*
and *respond* to the prompt that most speaks to you—or to the verse you

have already marked—and see what more God may reveal. The point is to follow where God is leading as you journey to peace. At the end of your journaling time, *pray* for God to embellish in your own heart, soul, and life the truths He has imparted. Ask for His strength and courage to go where He's leading you on the pathway to peace.

Within these pages, you have the opportunity to take hold of your God, life, voice, thoughts, purpose, dreams, spirit, study journal, and pen. *Trust* you will find the path, the clue, the word to be followed as peace finds its pathway to you.

Long life is in her right hand;
in her left hand are riches and honor.
Her ways are ways of pleasantness,
and all her paths are peace.
She is a tree of life to those who lay hold of her;
those who hold her fast are called blessed.
PROVERBS 3:16–18 ESV

SECTION 1: DEFINING AND FINDING PEACE

Peace begins with a smile.
MOTHER TERESA

Life can be chaotic, hectic, stressful, worrisome, and confounding. When you're coping with commitments, responsibilities, relationships, home life, and occasional crisis situations, it's easy to lose sight of the pathway to peace God has laid out before you. Yet once you slow down and make a point to understand and intentionally look for the comfort and tranquility God desires for and so freely offers to you, you will have that special serenity that comes only from your loving Creator.

In the thirty readings that follow, you will explore what God's peace is and how to find it. As you enter into God's Word, disregard any Bible commentary. This will allow God to speak to you one-on-one, heart-to-heart, Spirit-to-spirit, page-by-page. Begin with a prayer to God, something like "Here I am, Lord, a seeker of Your peace. Speak! I'm listening." Then read the scripture, expecting God to reveal Himself to you. Meditate on what you've read. Underline any words, phrases, or sentences that tug at your heart. Then quietly reflect on and honestly respond to the journaling prompts of your choice. Afterward, thank God for the moments you've shared, and ask Him to help you apply what you've learned to your spiritual life.

"Because of God's tender mercy, the morning light from heaven is
about to break upon us, to give light to those who sit in darkness
and in the shadow of death, and to guide us to the path of peace."
LUKE 1:78–79 NLT

PEACE ALONG YOUR WAY

Read Luke 1:78–79

Zacharias burst out in joyful song, proclaiming that because of God's love and mercy for His people, a Light—the "Sun of Righteousness" (Malachi 4:2 NLT)—was to rise and visit them, to dispel their darkness. How does physical light comfort you in the darkness? How does Jesus as your spiritual Light comfort you?

....

....

....

....

....

....

....

Jesus the Light is here to guide your "feet into the way of peace" (Luke 1:78–79 ESV). How does Jesus as the Word give you feet and help you find that path?

....

....

....

....

....

KEEPING CALM

—————————— *Read Psalm 94:1–13* ——————————

God knows human thoughts are futile. That's why those He instructs through His Word are blessed. How does God's Word change your thought life?

....

....

....

....

....

....

....

....

....

In what ways does knowing God's Word keep you "calm in the days of adversity" (Psalm 94:13 AMPC)?

....

....

....

....

....

A CONTINUAL GIFT

Read John 14:25–28

Jesus has gifted you His "peace of mind and heart" (John 14:27 NLT), a peace the world could never give. How does Jesus' gift to you keep on giving? How does Jesus' peace keep you from being troubled and afraid?

....

....

....

....

....

....

....

Jesus said the Holy Spirit would teach you everything and remind you of all Jesus has said. How often and in what ways does the Spirit teach you about and remind you of Jesus' peace?

....

....

....

....

....

....

....

ENTER THE PRINCE OF PEACE

Read Isaiah 9:1–7

You and the rest of the world were gifted with peace when Jesus was born. Even the angels admitted He would bring peace between you and God (Luke 2:14)! In what ways have you allowed Jesus to be the Prince of Peace in your life?

....

....

....

....

....

....

....

What part of your life might you be keeping from Jesus' rule?

....

....

....

....

....

....

....

PEACE BREAKS THROUGH

Read Luke 24:35–40; John 20:19–20

When you are emotionally, mentally, and spiritually locked in a room with your fears, in what ways does the calming presence of Jesus suddenly break through to bring you peace?

....

....

....

....

....

....

....

What do you feel Jesus needs to prove to you so that you can accept His peace wholeheartedly?

....

....

....

....

....

....

....

GOD'S BLESSING

Read Matthew 5:9

How do you, a woman of peace, promote or encourage peace in others?

....

....

....

....

....

....

....

....

Peacemakers are blessed because they are called children of God. In what ways might your peaceful actions result in more than that one blessing?

....

....

....

....

....

....

....

....

A CHARACTER OF GOD

Read 1 Thessalonians 5:23–24

Why might you find futile your efforts to make yourself holy? to make "your whole spirit and soul and body be kept blameless" (1 Thessalonians 5:23 ESV)?

....

....

....

....

....

....

....

How much of a relief is it that "the God of peace" will make you not just holy but blameless?

....

....

....

....

....

....

....

THE RULER OF HEARTS

Read Colossians 3:12–16

The peace of Christ is to rule in your heart, to govern over and control the entirely new you (Colossians 3:15 AMPC). How might you find it a challenge to let the peace of Christ act as umpire when other passions—such as anger, envy, jealousy, spite, etc.—threaten to usurp your calm?

....

....

....

....

....

....

....

How might turning to God's Word, singing spiritual songs, and being more thankful to God help you strengthen and empower your peace so that it can reign well over the new you?

....

....

....

....

....

....

TRANSCENDENT

Read Philippians 4:7

God's peace is "that tranquil state of a soul assured of its salvation through Christ, and so fearing nothing from God and being content with its earthly lot of whatever sort that is" (Philippians 4:7 AMPC). Are you cognizant of transcendent peace? Why or why not?

....

....

....

....

....

....

....

Amid what situations do you depend on God's peace guarding your heart and mind?

....

....

....

....

....

....

....

HARMONY, UNITY, AND UNDISTURBEDNESS

Read Ephesians 1:2–6

When, where, or with whom do you feel you most experience "grace (God's unmerited favor) and spiritual peace [which means peace with God and harmony, unity, and undisturbedness]" (Ephesians 1:2 AMPC)?

....

....

....

....

....

....

....

How do you feel knowing God chose you as His own to bless, save, and love even before the world was formed?

....

....

....

....

....

....

CALM CONFIDENCE IN GOD

Read Psalm 3

The amount of calm you have in your life is tied to your confidence in God. How might your lack of trust in God make you restless and perhaps too keyed up to sleep?

....

....

....

....

....

....

....

How might you increase your certainty and in turn your confidence that God indeed sustains you?

....

....

....

....

....

....

....

18

A BLESSING TIED TO STRENGTH

Read Psalm 29

Psalm 29's first ten verses extol God's strength, glory, and power. How might God's strength tie into your peace?

....

....

....

....

....

....

....

How might God's gifting you with His "[unyielding and impenetrable] strength" (Psalm 29:11 AMPC) give you peace?

....

....

....

....

....

....

....

....

IDENTIFIED WITH JESUS

Read 2 Thessalonians 3:16

In what ways does Jesus "the Lord of peace Himself grant you His peace (the peace of His kingdom)" (2 Thessalonians 3:16 AMPC)?

....

....

....

....

....

....

....

....

Does that peace stay with you "at all times and in all ways [under all circumstances and conditions, whatever comes]" (2 Thessalonians 3:16 AMPC)? Why or why not?

....

....

....

....

....

....

PEACE OF RECONCILIATION

Read Romans 5:1

How does it feel knowing you have been made right with God because of what Jesus has done for you?

....

....

....

....

....

....

....

....

How might that reconciliation give you unfathomable peace within and without?

....

....

....

....

....

....

....

TIED TO TRUST

Read Romans 15:13

Is your life lived knowing that "God, the source of hope, will fill you completely with joy and peace because you trust in him" (Romans 15:13 NLT)?

....

....

....

....

....

....

....

....

In what situations or environs might your trust find itself faltering and your peace dissipating?

....

....

....

....

....

....

....

PEACE IN SUBMITTING TO GOD

Read Job 22:21–22

Look deep within. Do you have some areas of your life in which you and God disagree? If so, what are they?

....

....

....

....

....

....

....

....

How might your agreeing with or submitting to God help you find peace? How might His Word lead you to find peace?

....

....

....

....

....

....

....

SLEEPING IN PEACE

Read Psalm 4

In what ways has God answered you when you called to Him (Psalm 4:1, 3)? How does knowing God hears and responds to your prayers help you find peace with and confidence in Him?

....

....

....

....

....

....

....

....

Try writing the words of Psalm 4:8 upon your heart and praying them back to the only One who can keep you safe. Might that help you get a good night's sleep?

....

....

....

....

....

....

RELEASED IN PEACE

Read Luke 2:25–35

Due to Simeon's devotion, the Holy Spirit was working in his life as He comforted him, communicated to him, and prompted him. How have you seen the Holy Spirit working in your life?

....

....

....

....

....

....

....

....

Once he'd realized his lifelong, Holy Spirit–promised reception of the Messiah, Simeon could die with peace in God's arms. What promise of peace are you awaiting from God?

....

....

....

....

....

....

THE PRIVILEGE OF PEACE

Read Romans 5:1–2

What has Jesus done that makes you right in God's eyes and given you peace with God?

....

....

....

....

....

....

....

....

Why might what you now have in Christ be labeled an "undeserved privilege" (Romans 5:2 NLT)?

....

....

....

....

....

....

....

RIGHTEOUSNESS AND PEACE

Read Isaiah 32:14–17

The prophet Isaiah predicts that the lives and lands of God's people will not be fruitful until what happens?

....

....

....

....

....

....

....

....

What will righteousness (right standing with God) bring (Isaiah 32:17)? How might that benefit your personal and spiritual life?

....

....

....

....

....

....

....

MOVING IN CLOSER

Read 1 Thessalonians 5:23; James 4:1–8

What moves people farther away from God? What moves *you* farther away from God?

....

....

....

....

....

....

....

....

How might moving closer to God change you and your world?

....

....

....

....

....

....

....

....

OPENING THE GATES

—————— *Read Psalm 24; 2 Thessalonians 3:16* ——————

In what ways do you feel you have "a right relationship with God" (Psalm 24:5 NLT), "the Lord of peace himself" (2 Thessalonians 3:16 NLT)?

....

....

....

....

....

....

....

....

What parts of your life might you have to open to God so that you can get closer to Him?

....

....

....

....

....

....

....

DIRECTLY INTO GOD'S PRESENCE

Read Hebrews 10:19–23; Romans 15:33

What allows you to enter into the presence of God?

....

....

....

....

....

....

....

....

....

What might you find yourself holding on to?

....

....

....

....

....

....

....

ASPECTS OF PEACE

Read 2 Peter 1:1–11

In what ways can God's grace and peace in you grow (2 Peter 1:2)?

....

....

....

....

....

....

....

....

God's peace is described as "perfect well-being, all necessary good, all spiritual prosperity, and freedom from fears and agitating passions and moral conflicts" (2 Peter 1:2 AMPC). List these from most to least in order of the aspects of peace you need.

....

....

....

....

....

....

PEACE INDWELLER

Read Ephesians 3:14–21

What prompts Jesus Christ to dwell in your heart?

....

....

....

....

....

....

....

....

....

How might Christ's presence within you and your knowledge of God's tremendous amount of love for you give you peace?

....

....

....

....

....

....

....

THE LOVE OF CHRIST

Read Romans 8:31–39

What things *cannot* separate you from God's love? Which of those things surprise you?

....

....

....

....

....

....

....

....

....

How might the knowledge you can never be separated from Christ's love give you the peace of God you crave?

....

....

....

....

....

....

FOR YOUR GOOD

Read Romans 8:26–28

When do you find it difficult to pray? Who comes to your aid when you don't know how to pray?

....

....

....

....

....

....

....

....

How might the knowledge that God is fitting things into a plan for your good help you find peace?

....

....

....

....

....

....

....

THE IDEA WOMAN

————— *Read Proverbs 19:21* —————

How do you feel when you have a few ideas but are not sure which you should choose?

....

....

....

....

....

....

....

....

How do you find peace in the knowledge that no matter which plan you choose, God's purpose will prevail?

....

....

....

....

....

....

....

ETERNAL ASSURANCE

Read Psalm 33

What comfort do you find in knowing you can trust whatever God does, no matter how your past or present circumstances appear?

....
....
....
....
....
....
....
....

How does knowing God's plans and intentions will never be shaken give you hope and peace?

....
....
....
....
....
....
....

A COVENANT OF PEACE

Read Ezekiel 34:25–31

List the many ways God has blessed you in this life.

....

....

....

....

....

How has God made you a blessing in the past? in the present?

....

....

....

....

....

What blessings do you believe await you in the life to come?

....

....

....

....

....

SECTION 2: CULTIVATING PEACE

Observe good faith and justice toward all nations.
Cultivate peace and harmony with all.
GEORGE WASHINGTON

It's great to read about peace, to study what it is and how to find it. But when you actually begin *cultivating* peace, it's an entirely new way of looking at your life as you actually begin to plant seeds of peace, carefully nurture the crop, and eventually reap God's calm within and without.

In the thirty readings that follow, you will explore various ways to cultivate God's peace. As you enter into His Word, remember to disregard any Bible commentary. Instead, allow God to speak to you directly, one-on-one, heart-to-heart, Spirit-to-spirit, page-by-page. Begin with a prayer to God, something like "Here I am, Lord, Your daughter and a seeker of Your peace. Speak! I'm listening." Then read the scripture, expecting God to reveal Himself to you. Meditate on what you've read. Underline any words, phrases, or sentences tugging at your heart. Then quietly reflect on and honestly respond to the journaling prompt(s) of your choice. Afterward, thank God for the moments you've shared, and ask Him to help you apply what you've learned as you embark upon the quest to cultivate His glorious peace.

"Because of God's tender mercy, the morning light from heaven
is about to break upon us, to give light to those who sit in darkness
and in the shadow of death, and to guide us to the path of peace."
LUKE 1:78–79 NLT

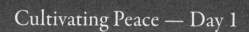

ADDING PEACE TO YOUR LIFE

Read Proverbs 3:1–2

How diligent are you in learning, memorizing, or keeping in your heart God's teachings and wisdom? How will doing all three lead you to a pathway to peace?

....

....

....

....

....

....

....

How does bowing to God's Word, will, and way add peace to your life? Bowing to which of the three Ws—Word, will, and way—is most challenging for you? Why?

....

....

....

....

....

....

....

DISTRACTIONS AND ENTANGLEMENTS: PART 1

———— Read Mark 10:46–52; Hebrews 12:1–2 ————

Distractions can keep you from not only reaching out to Jesus but from the peace that a connection with Him provides. Bartimaeus didn't allow the voices of others to distract him from calling to Jesus. What distractions might you have to turn a deaf ear or blind eye to?

....

....

....

....

....

....

How does your continual "looking away [from all that will distract] to Jesus" (Hebrews 12:2 AMPC) keep you on the road to His peace?

....

....

....

....

....

....

....

DISTRACTIONS AND ENTANGLEMENTS: PART 2

Read Mark 10:46–52; Hebrews 12:1–2

The blind Bartimaeus threw aside his cloak so that it would not trip him when he ran to Jesus. What item(s) may be threatening to entangle you as you run to Jesus?

....

....

....

....

How might you toss that cloak or "unnecessary weight" (Hebrews 12:1 AMPC) aside?

....

....

....

....

When your eyes are set on Jesus and all entanglements thrown aside, He'll ask you what you'd like Him to do for you. How will you answer that question?

....

....

....

TRUSTING GOD

Read Proverbs 3:5–6

How does trusting God, leaning on Him for everything, and being more confident in His wisdom than in your own put you on the pathway to peace?

....

....

....

....

....

....

....

....

In what areas of your life might you be forgetting to consult God or ignoring His advice? How has doing so kept you from His peace and your success?

....

....

....

....

....

....

....

ON EAGLES' WINGS

Read Exodus 19:1–5

After the Israelites had been enslaved in Egypt for four hundred years, God led them to freedom, telling them, "I carried you on eagles' wings and brought you to myself" (Exodus 19:4 NLT). How does that imagery of God's power and love for His people bring you peace?

....

....

....

....

....

....

....

How does it feel knowing that, by simple obedience to God, you too can be transformed as His treasure above all treasures? How does knowing He has a better plan for you increase your trust in His decisions for you?

....

....

....

....

....

....

THE NOBLER PATH

Read Romans 12:17–18

Paul says you're not to repay evil for evil but to take the nobler path. How might knowing that's your appropriate course of action help you keep calm when face-to-face with open hostility?

....

....

....

....

....

What measures have you taken to maintain peace with others?

....

....

....

....

How does knowing you can control only your own conduct help you find peace when conflict becomes unavoidable?

....

....

....

....

THE BEAUTY OF A PEACEFUL SPIRIT

Read 1 Peter 3:3–4

In what ways might you be more concerned with your outer self than with your inner, spiritual self?

....

....

....

....

God wants you to "clothe yourselves. . .with the beauty that comes from within, the unfading beauty of a gentle and quiet spirit" (1 Peter 3:4 NLT). Why do you think this is important to Him?

....

....

....

....

....

Like ripples in a pond, your peace can radiate to others, giving them peace. What can or do you do to radiate peace?

....

....

....

45

THE SEARCH FOR PEACE

Read 1 Peter 3:10–12

Why do you think happiness and peace go hand in hand?

....

....

....

....

....

....

....

....

In what ways do you search for peace? In what ways are you successful doing it? How do you maintain it?

....

....

....

....

....

....

....

....

PATHS OF PEACE

Read Proverbs 3:13–17

How do wisdom and understanding contribute to your joy?

....

....

....

....

....

....

....

....

About wisdom, the Bible says, "Her ways are pleasant, and all her paths, peaceful" (Proverbs 3:17 HCSB). Why do you think that is so? Do you find this to be true in your own life? Why or why not?

....

....

....

....

....

....

....

A SPIRIT OF CALM

Read 2 Timothy 1:6–12

In what ways do you find that God has not given you "a spirit of timidity (of cowardice, of craven and cringing and fawning fear)" but instead has given you "[a spirit] of power and of love and of calm and well-balanced mind and discipline and self-control" (2 Timothy 1:7 AMPC)?

....

....

....

....

....

....

....

....

How might knowing you actually have a spirit of calm within you increase your peace, no matter what arises in your life?

....

....

....

....

....

....

SHIELD AND PLACE OF SAFETY

Read Psalm 18:2, 19, 30, 35

The psalmist, David, sees God as "my shield, the power that saves me, and my place of safety" (Psalm 18:2 NLT). Then he relates how God proved that He was all those things in David's life. How has God proved to be all those things in your life?

....

....

....

....

....

....

....

How does God being your shield, standing between you and danger, being your place of safety, and keeping you out of harm's way give you peace about the present and the future?

....

....

....

....

....

....

LOVING GOD'S WORD, WILL, AND WAY

Read Psalm 119:105, 130, 165

About Psalm 119:165, *MacLaren's Expositions* says, "Base things loved always disturb. Noble things loved always tranquillise." In your own life, how has loving God's will given you the peace you long for?

....

....

....

....

....

....

....

....

How does God's Word keep you from stumbling along the way?

....

....

....

....

....

....

....

GREETINGS!

Read Romans 1:7

In his letters, Paul often greets readers with a blessing of grace and peace. *Grace* is God's unearned favor. *Peace* pertains to not just the absence of conflict but to a person being and living in harmony with God spiritually and physically; it also implies may all be well.

....

....

....

....

....

....

....

How might your life change if you invoked a blessing of grace and peace when greeting fellow believers? How might their lives change? How might the world change?

....

....

....

....

....

....

PEACE BY PEACE

Read 2 Corinthians 13:11

If people can find a way to live in peace with others, Paul reminds his readers, the God of peace and love will be present among them, spreading His love and peace within and without. When you are in conflict with others, does your inner peace escape you? Why or why not?

....

....

....

....

....

....

....

In what areas of your life are you experiencing conflict with others? How might those conflicts be resolved? What part might you need to play in resolving them?

....

....

....

....

....

....

EVERLASTING ARMS

Read Deuteronomy 33:27

What does running to God and using Him as your refuge look like to you?

....

....

....

....

....

What does it mean to have God's everlasting arms beneath you when you feel like you're in a free fall?

....

....

....

....

How might knowing God will catch you in midair give you more courage and less worry?

....

....

....

....

....

ANXIETY REMEDIES: PART 1

Read Philippians 4:6–7

The Word says you're to "not fret *or* have any anxiety about anything, but in every circumstance *and* in everything, by prayer and petition (definite requests), with thanksgiving, continue to make your wants known to God" (Philippians 4:6 AMPC). How might praying to God in every circumstance change your perspective of your circumstances? decrease your level of anxiety?

....

....

....

....

....

....

Why might peppering your prayers with thanksgiving and continuing to make your desires known to God keep you from needless worry?

....

....

....

....

....

....

ANXIETY REMEDIES: PART 2

Read Philippians 4:6–7

Paul says that if you follow the requirements of Philippians 4:6, "you will experience God's peace, which exceeds anything we can understand" (Philippians 4:7 NLT). When have you found that to be true for you?

....

....

....

....

What does God's peace look like to you?

....

....

....

....

Paul writes that God's "peace will guard your hearts and minds as you live in Christ Jesus" (Philippians 4:7 NLT). What does that mean to you? How important is that for your spiritual, mental, and emotional well-being?

....

....

....

....

RESURRECTION POWER

Read Ephesians 1:19–20

In what situation(s) have you discovered and finally understood "the incredible greatness of God's power" (Ephesians 1:19 NLT) because you believed?

....

....

....

....

....

....

....

....

How has that understanding of God's strength and resurrection power helped you keep your perspective, peace, and hope in times of trouble?

....

....

....

....

....

....

WELL OF HOPE

Read Genesis 21:15–19

Our actions can sometimes lead us into desperate situations in which all we want to do is sit down and cry. What do you do when hope seems to have deserted you? To whom do you look for help and comfort?

....

....

....

....

....

....

....

....

How might knowing that God is with you, no matter what you're going through, ease your anxiety? give you peace of mind? open your eyes to hope?

....

....

....

....

....

....

SHOULDER STRESS

Read Psalm 81:6–7

Stress can move into your shoulders, making them feel tight and stiff. But God is here to tell you, "Now I will take the load from your shoulders; I will free your hands from their heavy tasks" (Psalm 81:6 NLT). How might knowing God is ready to carry your burdens ease your tension?

....

....

....

....

....

....

....

Imagine, no matter where you are, God hears your cry and is ready to help you; answer you; ease your mind, body, spirit, and heart. What load can He help you carry, what questions can He answer for you today?

....

....

....

....

....

....

A HIDING PLACE

Read Psalm 32:7

How does knowing God can be a hiding place for you, a believer, give you ease?

....

....

....

....

Think of all the power, wonder, and strength He has shown in protecting you and others. How might that buoy your faith in worrisome situations?

....

....

....

....

....

How might God surrounding you with songs of victory and deliverance take you from worry to wonder? from fear to faith?

....

....

....

....

GOOD THINGS

Read Psalm 103:1–5

How might listing all the good things God does or has done for you boost your faith and lessen your worry?

....

....

....

....

....

....

....

At the end of each day, consider writing down all the things for which you are thankful. How might doing so change your perspective of that day? How might it make you feel as if your "youth is renewed like the eagle's" (Psalm 103:5 NLT)?

....

....

....

....

....

....

....

SLOW TO ANGER

Read Psalm 103:8–18

What are the chances that some of your anxiety comes from thinking you have failed God in some way?

....

....

....

....

....

....

....

God has too much compassion, mercy, and love for you to be upset with yourself for very long. What kind of relief does that provide for you? for others?

....

....

....

....

....

....

....

THE SECRET PLACE

Read Psalm 91:1–2

How do you envision the "secret place of the Most High" (Psalm 91:1 AMPC)?

....

....

....

....

How might your anxieties abate when you make it clear in your mind and engrave it upon your heart that you are safe "under the shadow of the Almighty [Whose power no foe can withstand]" (Psalm 91:1 AMPC)?

....

....

....

....

The psalmist sees God as his Refuge and Fortress, the one upon whom he leans, trusts, and relies. How do you see God? How does your vision of Him keep anxiety from overtaking you? What might you need to do to change how you see your Lord?

....

....

....

....

STRAIGHTENING UP

Read Luke 13:10–13

What weighs you down even when you enter your house of worship? How long have you tried to straighten up in your own power?

....

....

....

....

....

....

....

Jesus has compassion for you. He sees you and wants to release whatever is crippling you, keeping you from straightening up. What thing(s) would you like Jesus to release you from? What praise and thanks will you give Him?

....

....

....

....

....

....

....

IN HIS FOOTSTEPS: PART 1

Read Philippians 4:9

The apostle Paul had learned how to imitate Christ, how to follow in His footsteps. As Christ was Paul's example, Paul encouraged his readers to look to *him* as an example. In what ways do you believe you have been following in either Christ's or Paul's footsteps? In what areas have you strayed? Why?

....

....

....

....

....

....

....

What are the next steps you might want to take to help you become more like Jesus?

....

....

....

....

....

....

IN HIS FOOTSTEPS: PART 2

Read Philippians 4:7–9

When you practice the things learned from the apostle Paul, you'll not only have "the peace of God" (Philippians 4:7 ESV) but the "God of peace" (Philippians 4:9) Himself with you! What do you see as the difference between the two?

....

....

....

....

....

....

....

How might knowing peace is the result of your practice energize you and spur you on to becoming more and more like Christ? What might that "practice" look like?

....

....

....

....

....

....

SINGING OUT

Read Psalm 59

Although David was being continually harassed by King Saul, he found comfort and peace in singing praises to God. How might your singing "God is my Defense (my Protector and High Tower)" (Psalm 59:9 AMPC) give you peace even in the worst of circumstances?

....

....

....

....

....

....

....

What attributes of God give you the most peace when you remember them? Try writing a short song that you can sing to yourself to give you that special peace of God when you need it.

....

....

....

....

....

....

OPEN DOORS

Read Psalm 94:14–23

God has a way of bringing you comfort when you begin to have anxious thoughts—that's if you allow Him inside of not just your heart but your mind, soul, and spirit. Where might you need to open some doors so that God can enter and give you the peace you crave?

....

....

....

....

....

....

....

How much peace do you gain from knowing that even when your foot slips and you give yourself up for lost, God's hand of love is holding you up the entire time?

....

....

....

....

....

....

GOD'S GOODNESS

Read Psalm 27:13–14

How much more peace would you have in your life if you committed these words to your heart: "I am confident I will see the LORD's goodness while I am here in the land of the living" (Psalm 27:13 NLT)? How might the power of those words keep you in a place of peace during even the most difficult times?

....

....

....

....

....

....

....

Sometimes patience is required no matter where you are in life. How well could you calm your racing heart if you spoke the words of Psalm 27:14 into it?

....

....

....

....

....

SECTION 3: CHOOSING PEACE OVER PANDEMONIUM

Because of the favor of God,
we can have peace in the midst of chaos.
CRYSTAL MCDOWELL

Now that you know what peace is, how to find it, and how to cultivate it, it's time to look at how to choose peace over pandemonium. You can learn how to stop amid the chaos all around you, taking stock of who you are and who God is and choosing to respond with and in God's peace.

In the next thirty readings, you'll discover how to find God's peace and power no matter what is happening in your life. As you enter into His Word, remember to disregard any Bible commentary. Instead, allow God to speak to you directly, one-on-one, heart-to-heart, Spirit-to-spirit, page-by-page. Begin with a prayer to God, something like "Here I am, Lord, Your daughter and chooser of Your peace. Speak! I'm listening." Then read the scripture, expecting God to reveal Himself to you. Meditate on what you've read. Underline the words, phrases, or sentences tugging at your heart. Then quietly reflect on and honestly respond to the journaling prompt(s) of your choice. Afterward, thank God for the moments you've shared, and ask Him to help you apply what you've learned as you embark upon the quest to cultivate His glorious peace.

"Peace I leave with you; my peace I give to you. . . .
Let not your hearts be troubled, neither let them be afraid."
JOHN 14:27 ESV

PEACE GIVEN

Read John 14:27

In the first two sentences of verse 27, Jesus tells His followers that He is leaving them peace. That this isn't just any old peace, but *His* peace, as a sort of inheritance. Why was it so important for Jesus to leave His peace with all those who would follow Him, including you?

....

....

....

....

....

....

....

What is the difference between the peace of Jesus and the peace of the world? Which is more important to you?

....

....

....

....

....

....

....

PEACE CHOSEN

Read John 14:27

After Jesus tells His followers that He's leaving His own special kind of peace with them, He tells them, "Do not let your hearts be troubled, neither let them be afraid" (John 14:27 AMPC). In what ways do trouble and fear affect your God-given peace?

....

....

....

....

....

....

To make this verse clearer, the Amplified Bible, Classic Edition includes this text in brackets: "Stop allowing yourselves to be agitated and disturbed; and do not permit yourselves to be fearful and intimidated and cowardly and unsettled." How much is allowing your peace to be disrupted a choice on your part? How might the knowledge that maintaining peace is a choice help you keep your peace intact?

....

....

....

....

....

PEACE OF HEART

Read John 14:1

Jesus says, "Do not let your hearts be troubled (distressed, agitated). You believe in and adhere to and trust in and rely on God; believe in and adhere to and trust in and rely also on Me" (John 14:1 AMPC). How much does heart trouble disturb your peace?

....

....

....

....

....

....

In what ways do you think finding and maintaining your peace is connected to your trust in and reliance on not just Jesus but God and the Spirit? How would you rate your trust in Jesus, God, and the Holy Spirit? What can you do to increase that trust so that you can maintain your peace of heart?

....

....

....

....

....

....

CONFUSION VS. PEACE

Read 1 Corinthians 14:33

In his initial letter to Corinthians in the New Testament, Paul makes it clear who God is: "He. . .is not a God of confusion and disorder but of peace and order" (1 Corinthians 14:33 AMPC). How has God already proven that in the second verse of Genesis?

....

....

....

....

....

....

....

How much order and disorder do you have in your own life? Do you find that order leads to peace and disorder to chaos? Why or why not?

....

....

....

....

....

....

....

NOT YET READY

Read Exodus 13:17–18

You've decided to tackle a new endeavor, and you're looking for the easiest way to get from point A to point B. It looks like you're going to have to go the long way around. How might circuitous routes and dashed expectations disturb your peace?

....

....

....

....

....

....

God sees what you cannot. For example, He might see your way holds a challenge for which you are not yet ready. How might knowing God will help you find your way through the wilderness in His time and according to His map contribute to your overall sense of peace and well-being?

....

....

....

....

....

....

THE TWO SISTERS: PART 1

Read Luke 10:38–42

Martha welcomed Jesus into her house for dinner. What have you welcomed into your life that you, like Martha, later discovered took up more time and attention than you thought it would? What suffered because of that additional responsibility?

....

....

....

....

....

....

....

In what ways did you, like the overwrought Martha, end up whining to the Lord about decisions you had made?

....

....

....

....

....

....

....

THE TWO SISTERS: PART 2

Read Luke 10:38–42

On what occasions or under what circumstances did you feel other people may have thought you were lazy just because you'd decided to spend focused time with Jesus rather than get up and "do" as others were doing?

....

....

....

....

....

....

....

When have you felt you had the advantage over doers because you had chosen the better thing—spending quality time with Jesus?

....

....

....

....

....

....

....

THE TWO SISTERS: PART 3

Read Luke 10:38–42

What can you do in the future to keep yourself from allowing worldly cares and commitments—even those involving your family—to become more important than spiritual knowledge and times of being in the Lord's presence?

....

....

....

....

What steps can you take to make sure your focus is on the right thing(s)?

....

....

....

....

How might your feeling whiny, distracted, overwhelmed, or chaotic be a clue that something somewhere needs to be dropped and more time with Jesus taken up?

....

....

....

....

THE TWO SISTERS: PART 4

Read Luke 10:38–42

Who do you see yourself as—a distracted, overcommitted, and over-wrought Martha or a focused, freed, and peace-filled Mary? Have you always been that way? Why or why not?

....

....

....

....

What are you willing to do to become more of a Mary than a Martha? Who or what might stand in your way of taking those steps?

....

....

....

....

How might your spiritual life change when you find more time to sit at Jesus' feet? How welcome would that kind of change be in your eyes? in the eyes of others? in the eyes of Jesus?

....

....

....

....

CALM DURING CHAOS

Read Haggai 2:4–9

How confident are you that God stands in your midst not just during times of peace but during times of pandemonium?

....

....

....

....

....

How can you increase your confidence in God's abiding presence?

....

....

....

....

....

In the end, God promises peace and prosperity to His people, His house, and His land. In what ways have you already found His peace?

....

....

....

....

ANGEL ENCAMPMENTS

Read Psalm 34:1–7

When threatened by King Saul, David ran to Abimelech of Gath (Philistine territory) for protection. Then David had to pretend he was insane to escape Gath! So he cried out to God, who removed him from danger (1 Samuel 21:10–15). When has God delivered you from the danger created because you ran *away* from Him rather than *toward* Him?

....

....

....

....

....

....

....

In what ways did seeking God result in your being freed from all your fears and difficulties?

....

....

....

....

....

....

CRAVING PEACE

Read Psalm 34:10–14

Those who seek God lack no good thing. How has that been proven true in your life?

....

....

....

....

....

....

....

What actions do you take to turn away from the evil in your life? What actions do you take to do good? How successful are you?

....

....

....

....

....

....

....

....

PEACE PURSUERS

Read Psalm 34:15–20

When have you cried out in distress and the Lord has answered you? How did He help you?

....

....

....

....

....

In what ways did you feel God moving close when your heart was broken and you were crushed because of a misstep?

....

....

....

....

....

How does knowing God will always be there give you the peace you seek, crave, pursue, and ultimately receive from God?

....

....

....

SETTLING ACCOUNTS

Read Matthew 5:21–26

In what ways have you found your anger to be damaging to another? to you?

....

....

....

....

....

Who might you need to talk to and perhaps apologize to?

....

....

....

....

....

How will settling accounts with others give you the peace and freedom you seek in your life and in God's eyes?

....

....

....

....

ENTERING INTO PEACE

Read Luke 7:36–50

How do you demonstrate your love for Jesus, the forgiver of your sins?

....

....

....

....

....

How or when has His forgiveness of your misdeeds prompted you to weep?

....

....

....

....

....

How has your faith in Jesus' forgiveness helped you enter into the peace you crave?

....

....

....

....

IN THE MIDST OF FIRE: PART 1

Read Daniel 3

When have you, like Shadrach, Meshach, and Abednego, allowed your obedience to and faith in God to override any concerns you might have had about your personal safety, be it physical, spiritual, emotional, financial, or mental? (See Daniel 3:14–18.)

....

....

....

....

....

....

....

Where did you find the calm, faith, power, and fortitude to stand your ground even when threatened with dire consequences?

....

....

....

....

....

....

....

IN THE MIDST OF FIRE: PART 2

Read Daniel 3

What were the results of the choices you made when you resolved to remain obedient to God regardless of the consequences?

....

....

....

....

In what unexpected place did you discover Jesus walking with you amid the flames?

....

....

....

....

How did your actions due to your obedience to God change the people who witnessed your situation? How did your actions and the situation change you?

....

....

....

....

FOR PEACE

Read Psalm 120

In times of distress, when peace seems out of reach, to whom do you cry? How does an expectation of God answering you give you a sense of peace before, during, and after your prayer?

....

....

....

....

....

....

....

Verses 3 and 4 are addressed to the person disrupting the peace. Verses 5 and 6 pertain to the person of peace living amid ungodly people and also living far from God's house. When have you, a believer, felt alone among nonbelievers? How did you make it known that you were for peace?

....

....

....

....

....

....

WHATEVER AND ANYTHING

Read Philippians 4:8

One way to retain God's transcendent peace (Philippians 4:7) is to not just *think* about good things but to "fix your minds on them" (Philippians 4:8 AMPC). Having a list ahead of time, one you can keep in your Bible, could be a great help in this endeavor. Why not start a list now, writing one good thought for each item found in Philippians 4:8 (NLT)?

Whatever is true:

Whatever is honorable:

Whatever is right:

Whatever is pure:

Whatever is lovely:

Whatever is admirable:

Anything excellent:

Anything worthy of praise:

....

....

....

....

....

....

....

....

....

ELIJAH ON THE RUN: PART 1

Read 1 Kings 19

On what occasion(s) have you found yourself fleeing into the wilderness to hide?

....

....

....

....

When have you been so tired, depressed, and afraid that you plopped down underneath a broom tree and told God you'd "had enough" (1 Kings 19:4 NLT)?

....

....

....

....

How did God answer your plea?

....

....

....

....

....

ELIJAH ON THE RUN: PART 2

Read 1 Kings 19

In what miraculous way did God provide for you during your broom-tree experience?

....

....

....

....

....

What angels has God sent into your life to minister to you, touch you, provide for you when peace seemed out of reach?

....

....

....

....

In what ways did God give you the direction you needed to find your way out of the wilderness and the strength you needed to travel?

....

....

....

....

ELIJAH ON THE RUN: PART 3

Read 1 Kings 19

When has God told you to "go back the same way you came" (1 Kings 19:15 NLT) instead of running away from the situation? How did that work out for you? for others?

....

....

....

....

....

....

....

In what ways did God's ferreting out the truth(s) of your situation change your attitude toward it? How did God help you reclaim your peace and help you move forward—for Him, in truth—once more?

....

....

....

....

....

....

....

MATERIAL POSSESSIONS

Read Luke 12:13–21

What items have you purchased recently that you haven't yet used or ended up giving or throwing away?

....

....

....

....

How can a burning desire for material things you don't really need but definitely want eat away at your peace? keep you from having a richer relationship with God?

....

....

....

....

What steps can you take to invest more in your spiritual life than your material life?

....

....

....

....

YOUR WORTH: PART 1

Read Luke 12:6–7

Jesus says that although five sparrows are sold for two pennies, "not one of them is forgotten or uncared for in the presence of God" (Luke 12:6 AMPC). How does that comfort you?

....
....
....
....
....
....
....

Jesus says that "the very hairs of your head are all numbered" (Luke 12:7 AMPC). How does this help you to "not be struck with fear or seized with alarm" (Luke 12:7 AMPC)? How does it bring the peace you seek?

....
....
....
....
....
....
....

YOUR WORTH: PART 2

Read Luke 12:6–7

How might knowing how valuable you are to God help you see the value others have in His eyes?

....

....

....

....

....

....

....

....

How does Jesus' view of your worth differ from the world's view of your worth? Which view gives you more peace?

....

....

....

....

....

....

....

PEACE DISRUPTORS

Read Luke 12:22–32

In what ways might you find yourself depending more upon your paycheck than God?

....

....

....

....

....

What steps can you take to become more focused on the fact that God *will* provide for you rather than worrying about how He's going to do it?

....

....

....

....

What does Jesus encourage you to aim for and seek, knowing that when you do that, your needs will be provided?

....

....

....

....

FINDING AND KEEPING PEACE

Read Psalm 46

How does knowing where God is (with you) and who He is (your Refuge, Strength, Fortress, Stronghold, and Hightower) help you when the earth changes, causing mountains to shake and fall into the seas? How does that give you hope?

....

....

....

....

....

....

God tells you, "Let be and be still, and know (recognize and understand) that I am God" (Psalm 46:10 AMPC). How might writing those words on your mind and heart help you to obtain, maintain, and retain your peace in times of trouble?

....

....

....

....

....

....

WINGED DELIVERER

Read Psalm 91:1–8

To whom do you turn or where do you go when you need refuge from the storms of emotions, hormones, or illnesses that come your way?

....

....

....

In many scriptures, reference is made to God sheltering His followers beneath His wings (Ruth 2:12; Matthew 23:37; Psalm 17:8; etc.). How does that image of God's love and protection give you peace in times of trouble or sorrow?

....

....

....

....

Psalm 91:8 (AMPC) says you can consider yourself "inaccessible in the secret place of the Most High." How would it feel to be there, sheltered and unable to be reached by trouble or troublemakers? What might you do to find your way there?

....

....

....

IN ANGELS' CHARGE

Read Psalm 91:9–12

How do you make God your refuge and a place where you dwell on a regular basis? What does *regular* mean to you? Is that often enough?

....
....
....
....
....
....
....

Wherever you go, God's angels go, providing a constant wall and shield of protection around you. How does knowing that give you peace in these days?

....
....
....
....
....
....
....

LOVE AND TRUST

Read Psalm 91:13–16

God says He will rescue all those who love Him and trust in His name. How do you show your love to God? How do you show Him your trust in Him?

....

....

....

....

In what ways is it obvious to those around you that you love and trust God?

....

....

....

....

God is your rescuer and protector. He's the one who runs to help you when you call His name. How does knowing He can and will do everything for you give you peace of mind and heart?

....

....

....

....

....

SECTION 4: STAYING CALM AMID THE STORMS

If God be our God, He will give us peace in trouble. When there is a storm without, He will make peace within. The world can create trouble in peace, but God can create peace in trouble.
THOMAS WATSON

One of the biggest challenges is keeping your peace amid the storms, amid the chaos swirling around you. That's what these next thirty readings are all about.

In the following readings, you'll discover how to stay calm through the fiercest storms in your life. As you delve into His Word, remember to disregard any Bible commentary. Simply allow God to speak to you. Begin by praying, "Here I am, good Teacher, Your student. Help me learn how to keep calm amid life's storms. Speak, Lord! I'm listening." Then read the scripture, expecting God to reveal Himself. Meditate on what you've read. Mark the words, phrases, or sentences tugging at your heart. Then quietly reflect on and truthfully respond to the journaling prompt(s) of your choice. Afterward, thank God for the moments you've shared, and ask Him to help you apply what you've learned as you embark upon the quest to keep calm no matter how strong the storm.

He arose and rebuked the wind and said to the sea, Hush now! Be still (muzzled)! And the wind ceased (sank to rest as if exhausted by its beating) and there was [immediately] a great calm (a perfect peacefulness).
MARK 4:39 AMPC

A SHELTER FROM THE STORM

Read Isaiah 25:4

In what situation(s) might you have been the maker of the storm in your life? When have you been an innocent bystander into whose life a seemingly random storm blew? How might you have handled these storms differently?

....

....

....

....

....

What lessons have your storms taught you?

....

....

....

....

How has Jesus proven to be your shelter from your storms?

....

....

....

....

STILLING THE STORM: PART 1

Read Mark 4:35–41

When have you followed Jesus' command to launch out to sea, only to find yourself soon being pounded by waves amid a terrible storm?

....

....

....

....

In what ways might your feelings of fear and panic manifest around you as you found yourself battling this unexpected storm?

....

....

....

....

When, if ever, did you believe Jesus might be neglecting you, sleeping on the job, just when you needed Him most?

....

....

....

....

....

STILLING THE STORM: PART 2

Read Mark 4:35–41

Stop and consider how awesome it was that Jesus "arose and rebuked the wind and said to the sea, Hush now! Be still (muzzled)! And the wind ceased (sank to rest as if exhausted by its beating) and there was [immediately] a great calm (a perfect peacefulness)" (Mark 4:39 AMPC). Write down any thoughts and feelings this passage prompts within you.

....

....

....

....

....

....

Jesus, Lord of the wind and waves, chided His disciples' feelings of fear and their anxiety of His abandoning them. When might He have wanted to do the same to you?

....

....

....

....

....

....

HANNAH'S STORM: PART 1

Read 1 Samuel 1

What was the storm that had blown into Hannah's life?

....

....

....

....

Who had been the generator of her storm? (See verse 5.) What made Hannah's storm even more difficult to bear?

....

....

....

....

....

Why might she have been unable to find comfort from her husband's words and his love of her?

....

....

....

....

....

HANNAH'S STORM: PART 2

Read 1 Samuel 1

What prompted Hannah, distressed and weeping bitterly, to finally go to the Lord and pray over her situation?

....

....

....

....

....

What role did Hannah's vow and prayer to God play in the making of her son and the remaking of her?

....

....

....

....

When have you poured your life out to God and then walked away relieved?

....

....

....

....

....

HANNAH'S STORM: PART 3

Read 1 Samuel 1

When in your life did God intentionally put a storm in your path, denying you something, then, when the time was right, granting your request? Why do you think He allowed that storm?

....

....

....

....

....

How did you celebrate God's removal of your storm by changing your situation or finally granting your request?

....

....

....

....

What have you learned from the storms God has allowed in your life?

....

....

....

....

WATER WALKERS: PART 1

Read Matthew 14:22–33

When have you followed Jesus' directions only to find yourself soon afterward in a huge storm?

....

....

....

....

....

When has Jesus come to you amid a storm before you even cried out for help?

....

....

....

....

When have you taken the courage that Jesus offers you when you're in distress? How does knowing that He exists boost your confidence in Him?

....

....

....

....

WATER WALKERS: PART 2

Read Matthew 14:22–33

In what ways have you shown you're just as courageous as Peter by stepping out of your boat, the S.S. *Comfort Zone*, and walking on the water to Jesus?

....

....

....

....

What happens when you take your eyes off Jesus and look at the wind and waves?

....

....

....

....

How might the peace that followed your rescue convince you that your lifesaver was indeed Jesus?

....

....

....

....

THEIR DESIRED HAVEN

Read Psalm 107:23–31

In what ways have you found your wisdom to be of no help in delivering yourself from storms?

....

....

....

....

How confident are you that God can do anything, including saving you from storm after storm?

....

....

....

....

How does it make you feel to know that once God rescues you from the storm, you will find joy in the calm and immediately afterward He will bring you to your "desired haven" (Psalm 107:30 AMPC)?

....

....

....

....

THE LORD IS PEACE: PART 1

Read Judges 6:1–24

The Lord greets Gideon, who is hiding from the Midianites, by saying, "Mighty hero, the LORD is with you!" (Judges 6:12 NLT). When has God called you by an attribute you had yet to display or to recognize within yourself?

....

....

....

In what circumstances have you asked God, "If the LORD is with us, why has all this happened to us? And where are all the miracles our ancestors told us about?" (Judges 6:13 NLT).

....

....

....

....

God said to Gideon, "Go with the strength you have, and rescue Israel from the Midianites. I am sending you!" (Judges 6:14 NLT). God ascribes strength to Gideon, implying that because He is sending him, He will also equip him. In what ways has God equipped you before sending you?

....

....

....

THE LORD IS PEACE: PART 2

Read Judges 6:1–24

Instead of being encouraged by God's vision of him, Gideon explains why he's not a qualified candidate. When have you made similar excuses to God about why you cannot do as He asks?

....

....

....

God explains that the difference between a weak Gideon and a strong Gideon is His presence. How does God being with you change your thoughts and feelings about your own strength and power?

....

....

....

When God says to Gideon, "Peace be to you. Do not fear; you shall not die" (Judges 6:23 ESV), he builds an altar to God and names it the Lord is Peace. How has God proven to you that His presence is not death but life and peace?

....

....

....

....

RECOVERY

Read 1 Samuel 30:1–20

Having lost all—home, hearth, family, friends, and comrades—David turned to God for encouragement and strength. Where and to whom do you go for encouragement and strength when all seems lost?

....

....

....

....

....

What next steps do you take to recover what you've lost? Whose wisdom might you seek?

....

....

....

....

What was the result? What different steps might you take the next time?

....

....

....

....

TRUSTING JESUS' WORD

Read Luke 5:1–10

When has Jesus told you to go deeper?

....

....

....

....

In what ways did you then trust Jesus at His word? What was the result?

....

....

....

....

....

How did the results of trusting Jesus' word against all reason transform your frustration into desired peace and inspired worship?

....

....

....

....

....

PERIL, PRAYER, PLUNDER, AND PEACE: PART 1

——————— *Read 2 Chronicles 20:1–30* ———————

Having received news that three armies were coming to invade his kingdom, a fearful Jehoshaphat set his face to seek the Lord. When you receive frightening news, whom do you turn to first? Whom do you ask to join you in your quest for guidance?

....

....

....

Jehoshaphat admits to God, "We are powerless against this great horde that is coming against us. We do not know what to do, but our eyes are on you" (2 Chronicles 20:12 ESV). When have you prayed such a prayer, humbling yourself by reminding yourself who God is, who you are, and how dependent you are on Him?

....

....

....

....

How might a person who prays such a prayer appear in God's eyes?

....

....

....

PERIL, PRAYER, PLUNDER, AND PEACE: PART 2

Read 2 Chronicles 20:1–30

What peace do you gain knowing your battles aren't yours but God's?

....
....
....
....

Instead of taking things into your own hands, how hard might it be for you to stand still, hold your position, and watch God work things out? What might make doing those things easier for you?

....
....
....
....
....

How does it feel knowing that no matter what you face, God is with you?

....
....
....
....

PERIL, PRAYER, PLUNDER, AND PEACE: PART 3

——————— *Read 2 Chronicles 20:1–30* ———————

After hearing the words of the Lord, King "Jehoshaphat bowed his head with his face to the ground" (2 Chronicles 20:18 ESV)—and he did so in front of his people! How might such a display of humility change him? change his people? change you?

....

....

....

The next morning, before the battle commenced, Jehoshaphat told his people, "Believe in the LORD your God, and you will be able to stand firm. Believe in his prophets, and you will succeed" (2 Chronicles 20:20 NLT). How does your faith and trust in God play a role in your own battles?

....

....

....

Jehoshaphat instructed singers to walk before his army and sing praises to God! Have you ever done the same thing while walking into what others might perceive as danger?

....

....

....

PERIL, PRAYER, PLUNDER, AND PEACE: PART 4

Read 2 Chronicles 20:1–30

"The moment they began their shouts and praises, the LORD set an ambush" (2 Chronicles 20:22 HCSB) against the enemy armies. What does this tell you about the power of praise?

....

....

....

By the time Jehoshaphat and his people got to the battlefield, all that remained was to gather the plunder. How might that give you a new perspective on holding on to your peace and praising amid possible peril?

....

....

....

....

After this amazing battle, "Jehoshaphat's kingdom was at peace" (2 Chronicles 20:30 NLT). How might this study of Peril, Prayer, Plunder, and Peace help you find your way to victory when facing conflict?

....

....

....

A FAITHFUL HABIT: PART 1

Read Daniel 6

Would others consider you "faithful, always responsible, and completely trustworthy" (Daniel 6:4 NLT)? Why or why not?

....

....

....

....

....

....

....

On what occasions have others discovered that what they'd considered your biggest weakness—your faith—was actually your greatest strength? When have *you* discovered your faith to be your greatest strength?

....

....

....

....

....

....

....

A FAITHFUL HABIT: PART 2

Read Daniel 6

When, if ever, have you hidden yourself away to pray, regardless of laws or the opinions of others?

....

....

....

....

....

In what ways has your prayer routine become your usual practice regarding time, place, etc.? How do you think a person's prayer practice tends to promote peace within?

....

....

....

....

How might you make your prayer practice more of a faithful habit?

....

....

....

....

A FAITHFUL HABIT: PART 3

Read Daniel 6

In what ways has or does your trust in God keep you unharmed, able to sleep, and at peace regardless of your circumstances?

....

....

....

....

....

How might your life of trust and peace in God demonstrate your Lord's saving power?

....

....

....

....

How might your life of trust and peace in God help you prosper?

....

....

....

....

....

THE RED SEA EXPERIENCE: PART 1

Read Exodus 14

When have you felt that the predicament in which you found yourself was not of your own making but brought about by God alone?

....

....

....

....

When have you been sandwiched between a rock and a hard place with no feasible way out? When would you have gladly gone back and retraced your steps to get out of your untenable position?

....

....

....

....

How might you have vocally complained to God before you realized what you were doing, questioned His plan, or began devising a plan of your own? If so, what prompted you to do so?

....

....

....

....

THE RED SEA EXPERIENCE: PART 2

Read Exodus 14

When God's people were trapped between the Egyptians and the Red Sea, Moses gave them some very inspiring words in Exodus 14:13–14. In situations where your faith is mightily tested, what effect would those words have on you?

....

....

....

....

What would standing firm look like to you?

....

....

....

....

What would it feel like to believe that the trouble you see today you would never see again? What kind of peace would that bring you?

....

....

....

....

THE RED SEA EXPERIENCE: PART 3

Read Exodus 14

When have you felt as if the angel of God was guarding you from behind as you moved forward?

....

....

....

What peace does the knowledge that God has your back give you? What courage does it give you to keep moving forward?

....

....

....

When have you felt as if, because of God, you were walking on dry ground while all those against you were swept away by the sea?

....

....

....

How have your own Red Sea experiences given you not just a boost of faith but peace of mind?

....

....

BELIEF VS. FEAR: PART 1

Read Mark 5:21–24, 35–43

When have you been so distressed that you went to Jesus and just fell at His feet, pleading for His help?

....

....

....

....

....

When, if ever, have you had a feeling that your answer to prayer was delayed?

....

....

....

....

How confident are you that Jesus will help you based on *His* timetable not yours? What peace does that give you?

....

....

....

....

BELIEF VS. FEAR: PART 2

Read Mark 5:21–24, 35–43

When have you prayed with the feeling that any answer or help from Jesus would come too late?

....

....

....

....

What reassurance and peace do Jesus' words "Do not fear, only believe" (Mark 5:36 ESV) give you? When has Jesus challenged you to believe no matter how dire the situation appeared?

....

....

....

....

What might you be willing to do to live in God's peace no matter what your apprehensions or challenges?

....

....

....

....

A WOMAN WITH ISSUES: PART 1

Read Mark 5:25–34

In what ways might you be putting all your faith (and perhaps money) into a remedy other than Jesus to rid yourself of a constant and long-term malady? How might doing so steal your peace?

....

....

....

....

When have you, in desperation, gone beyond societal, familial, or seemingly rational norms and reached out to Jesus, knowing He is your only hope? What prompted you to do so?

....

....

....

....

What methods do you use to encourage yourself to reach out to Jesus?

....

....

....

....

A WOMAN WITH ISSUES: PART 2

Read Mark 5:25–34

When have you ever been instantly healed or transformed after reaching out to Jesus in faith?

....

....

....

....

In this reading, "Jesus realized at once that healing power had gone out from him" (Mark 5:30 NLT). When have you realized that Jesus' healing power had entered you? What was that feeling like?

....

....

....

....

Jesus told this woman with the issue of blood, "Daughter, your faith has made you well. Go in peace. Your suffering is over" (Mark 5:34 NLT). How does your faith make you well? give you peace? end your suffering?

....

....

....

....

JOSEPH'S JOURNEYS: PART 1

Read Genesis 39

What have adversities in your life taught you?

....

....

....

....

Even amid trying times, what has recognizing God's presence in your life led you to?

....

....

....

....

....

What can make you a peace-filled and prosperous woman, despite *ongoing* adverse circumstances?

....

....

....

....

....

JOSEPH'S JOURNEYS: PART 2

Read Genesis 40–41

In what ways do you give God credit for whatever wisdom you may have?

....

....

....

....

How do you keep a positive mind-set when people break their promises to you and, because of those broken promises, your adverse circumstances continue?

....

....

....

....

....

If you continually give God credit for all things, how might this not only please God but benefit you?

....

....

....

....

JOSEPH'S JOURNEYS: PART 3

Read Genesis 43; 50

What allowed Joseph to extend kindness to his brothers rather than the scolding they may have deserved?

....

....

....

....

In what situations have you, like Joseph, found a way to retain your peace? What gave you the strength and heart to do so?

....

....

....

....

Joseph told his brothers, "You intended to harm me, but God intended it all for good. He brought me to this position so I could save the lives of many people" (Genesis 50:20 NLT). How does this truth help you find peace in your life?

....

....

....

....

SECTION 5: KEEPING YOUR PEACE WHEN. . .

Knowing how to keep your peace within and without is crucial to growing in Christ. Thus, in the sixty readings that follow, you will be given anxiety-laden "when" scenarios along with words of God to counter any peace-disrupting thoughts you may find yourself entertaining and to help you realign your own thinking with God's.

Before delving into these readings, pray, perhaps something like "Show me, Lord, how to see my situations through Your eyes and how to replace any erroneous thoughts I have with *Your* thoughts so that I may keep Your peace."

After completing your Bible study questions for the day, thank God for the moments you've shared with Him. Then ask Him to help you compose a Personal Peace Prayer, one that will help you quickly alter your thoughts to more closely reflect His the next time(s) the need arises.

May this section be a guide you can turn to again and again, making it an invaluable aid for living an anxiety-free life for years to come.

We are human, but we don't wage war as humans do. We use
God's mighty weapons, not worldly weapons, to knock down the
strongholds of human reasoning and to destroy false arguments.
We destroy every proud obstacle that keeps people from knowing God.
We capture their rebellious thoughts and teach them to obey Christ.
2 CORINTHIANS 10:3–5 NLT

WHEN LONELY

Read 2 Timothy 4:9–22

In what ways, if any, do you think you have been deserted?

....

....

....

How has God stood by you? What gifts has He given you by doing so?

....

....

....

How does knowing God will always stick by you help you retain your peace this side of heaven?

....

....

....

....

Personal Peace Prayer

....

....

....

WHEN SLEEPLESS

Read Proverbs 3:24–26; Psalm 3:5; 4:8

What fears have been keeping you up lately? What solutions does God offer that will give you the good night's sleep you need?

....

....

....

....

....

In what ways does God keep you safe so you can lie down and sleep in peace? How will you engrave this information on your mind so you can continue to rest in God's peace at night?

....

....

....

....

....

Personal Peace Prayer

....

....

....

WHEN AGGRAVATED

—— *Read Proverbs 12:16; Ephesians 4:2; Psalm 37:8–9* ——

In what ways can staying "calm when insulted" (Proverbs 12:16 NLT) not only be the godly thing to do but the wise thing to do?

....

....

....

Which do you do more often, accept the faults of others, bearing with them in love, or become aggravated with them? Why do you think God would prefer you love others no matter what?

....

....

....

When has your temper led to you harming yourself? others? God?

....

....

....

Personal Peace Prayer

....

....

....

WHEN DEPRESSED

Read Numbers 21:4–9

Disappointment, frustration, hopelessness, and exhaustion all worked together to deeply depress the spirits of the Israelites who'd been wandering in the wilderness for thirty-eight years. What did their depression prompt them to do?

....

....

....

In what ways might you follow the same pattern—disappointment, frustration, hopelessness, exhaustion, depression, and grumbling—in your life?

....

....

The Israelites had forgotten how God had preserved and provided for them for thirty-eight years. What blessings might you be forgetting?

....

....

....

Personal Peace Prayer

....

....

WHEN IN HIDING

—————————— *Read Judges 6* ——————————

When, where, and why do you sometimes hide when the going gets tough?

....

....

....

God told Gideon who he was, what he was capable of, before Gideon himself knew! What might God tell you about yourself right now?

....

....

....

Just as God was with Gideon (Judges 6:16), He is with you. Why is that important?

....

....

....

Personal Peace Prayer

....

....

....

WHEN ANGRY

—— *Read Matthew 5:22; James 1:19–20; Ephesians 4:26–31* ——

How can being angry make you a fool or get you into big trouble?

....

....

....

When have you let the sun go down on your anger? What did that lead to?

....

....

....

What advice does James supply so God-followers can avoid the pitfalls created by anger?

....

....

....

Personal Peace Prayer

....

....

....

....

WHEN UNDER STRESS

Read 1 Kings 19

When under great stress, the fight, flight, or freeze response—your body's natural reaction to perceived danger—kicks in. When Queen Jezebel threatened Elijah, he literally ran for his life. What's your usual reaction to danger?

....

....

....

How does God minister to you during times of great stress?

....

....

....

What steps do you take so you can hear God's voice in the stillness?

....

....

....

Personal Peace Prayer

....

....

....

WHEN UNSURE OF GOD'S PROVISION

*———— Read Genesis 22:1–14; Malachi 3:10; ————
Matthew 6:33; 7:7–11; Philippians 4:19*

When has God brought you to the brink only to provide for you at the last minute?

....

....

....

When it comes to provision, what is your first responsibility? What does Jesus encourage you to do? What does Paul say God will do?

....

....

....

What other verses can shore up your faith that God will indeed provide for all your needs?

....

....

....

Personal Peace Prayer

....

....

WHEN IN A DIFFICULT SITUATION

Read Joshua 6:3; Judges 7:7; 1 Kings 17:9, 13

When you're in what appears to be a difficult situation, you can always count on God to do the impossible. Why does God sometimes call you to do what goes against your reasoning, just as He did with Joshua, Gideon, and Elijah?

....

....

....

What do their stories teach you about God? about yourself? about walking in faith?

....

....

Even Jesus was tested. How does that make you feel about your own difficulties?

....

....

....

Personal Peace Prayer

....

....

WHEN WAITING

Read Psalm 25:5; 27:14; 62:5; 123:2

David waited for guidance from God, telling Him, "for You [You only and altogether] do I wait [expectantly] all the day long" (Psalm 25:5 AMPC). Do you wait for God with the expectation that He will come through for you? Why or why not?

....

....

....

....

What do Psalm 27:14, Psalm 62:5, and Psalm 123:2 tell you about how to be and what to do while you're waiting on God?

....

....

....

....

Personal Peace Prayer

....

....

....

....

WHEN FRUSTRATED

—— *Read Ecclesiastes 7:9; Colossians 3:12–13; Galatians 6:9* ——

Frustration ends up leading, in most cases, to anger. Yet Ecclesiastes 7:9 (ESV) tells us "anger lodges in the heart of fools." When has your frustration led you to do something foolish?

....

....

....

What ideas does Colossians 3:12–13 give you about keeping frustration from flaring up?

....

....

....

What will help you to keep on keeping on, no matter how frustrated you get?

....

....

....

Personal Peace Prayer

....

....

WHEN BURDENED

—— *Read Psalm 55:22; Matthew 11:28–30; 1 Peter 5:6–7* ——

How might your clinging to a burden cause you to slip and fall?

....

....

What does His rest, ease, relief, and refreshment look like to you?

....

....

Why are Jesus' teachings (the burden or yoke He gives you) lighter than those of the rabbis' teachings? Which burden—the teaching of Jesus or of rabbis—would you rather carry?

....

....

....

Why does God want you to give Him all your anxieties and cares? When was the last time you did so?

....

....

Personal Peace Prayer

....

....

WHEN IN TROUBLE

Read Psalm 34:17; 50:15; 121

What does God expect you to do after He rescues you?

....

....

....

Where do you look when you're in trouble? To the hills where God resides or somewhere else?

....

....

....

....

What will God do for you when you look for and cry out to Him?

....

....

....

Personal Peace Prayer

....

....

....

WHEN TIRED

—— *Read 1 Kings 8:56; Jeremiah 31:25; Isaiah 40:11, 29* ——

How does knowing God will always make good on His promises help you rest?

....

....

....

Picture God protecting you, feeding you, gently leading you, and gathering you up in His arms to carry you. How does that make you feel?

....

....

....

When has God come along and given you power and increased your strength? How has that given you a new and stronger grip on life?

....

....

....

Personal Peace Prayer

....

....

....

WHEN ANXIOUS

—————— Read Numbers 6:22–27 (Aaron's Blessing) ——————

God has promised to bless you and "watch, guard, and keep you" (Numbers 6:24 AMPC). How might knowing that make you less anxious?

....

....

....

When has God smiled upon you or been kind, merciful, and gracious to you? What did that look or feel like?

....

....

....

How does God continually look upon you with favor and give you "peace (tranquility of heart and life continually)" (Numbers 6:26 AMPC)?

....

....

....

Personal Peace Prayer

....

....

....

WHEN FACING DANGER

Read 2 Samuel 20:14–22

When her city of Abel was under attack, the wise woman first figured out who was in charge. Then she asked him to listen to what she had to say. What were the first things you did when faced with danger?

....

....

....

In what ways do you let those who are threatening you know you are "peace loving and faithful" (2 Samuel 20:19 NLT)? How might that help defuse the situation?

....

....

How might you use the wise woman's tactics—without cutting off anyone's head—in today's society?

....

....

....

Personal Peace Prayer

....

....

WHEN WORRIED ABOUT THE FUTURE

Read Proverbs 3:5–6

How does trusting in the Lord help you lay aside your worries about the future?

....

....

....

Why are you advised not to "rely on your own insight or understanding" (Proverbs 3:5 AMPC)?

....

....

....

How do you go about finding God's will and what path He would have you take?

....

....

....

Personal Peace Prayer

....

....

....

WHEN IN DOUBT

———— Read Romans 4:20–21; Mark 9:24 ————

How might having full confidence in God make you grow strong and empowered by faith?

....

....

....

How assured are you that God is "able and mighty to keep His word and to do what He had promised" (Romans 4:21 AMPC)? What steps might you take to increase that assurance?

....

....

....

When have you prayed, "Lord, I believe! [Constantly] help my weakness of faith" (Mark 9:24 AMPC)? How did God answer that prayer?

....

....

....

Personal Peace Prayer

....

....

WHEN NOT SURE HOW TO PRAY

Read Romans 8:26–27

When have you gone to pray but stumbled over your words, having no idea how to pray? How does the Holy Spirit go "to meet" (Romans 8:26 AMPC) you when you cannot find the words to pray?

....

....

....

....

How does knowing that God has provided you with this holy interceder change the way you think about prayer and the entity to whom you are praying?

....

....

....

....

Personal Peace Prayer

....

....

....

....

WHEN DISCOURAGED

Read Joshua 1:5–9

Why do you think God tells Joshua to be strong and courageous three times (Joshua 1:6, 7, 9)?

....

....

....

How might knowing that God will be with you wherever you go and will never fail you keep you from becoming discouraged?

....

....

....

Why is it important to meditate on God's Word day and night? How might that give you success and keep you from becoming discouraged?

....

....

....

Personal Peace Prayer

....

....

....

151

WHEN FEELING HELPLESS

Read Isaiah 41:8–13

What is the reason you need not fear?

....

....

....

How does God strengthen you and hold you up?

....

....

....

How do you feel knowing that you'll never again see those who are against you? How do you feel knowing that God is holding your right hand, telling you to not fear, that *He*—the Lord of all—will help you?

....

....

....

Personal Peace Prayer

....

....

....

WHEN IN NEED OF REST

———— Read Jeremiah 6:16; Matthew 11:28; Mark 6:31 ————

When was the last time you stood at a crossroad, looked around, asked for the old, godly way, and walked in it? How did that help you find rest for your soul?

....

....

....

Jesus promises to "ease and relieve and refresh your souls" (Matthew 11:28 AMPC). How and when do you allow Him to do so?

....

....

....

How might going away by yourself to a deserted place with Jesus help you find the rest you need? When, where, and how might you do so?

....

....

....

Personal Peace Prayer

....

....

153

WHEN FACED WITH THE IMPOSSIBLE

——— *Read Jeremiah 32:17; Mark 9:23; Ephesians 3:20* ———

God continually proves He can do the impossible (see Genesis 18:14; Joshua 10:12–14)! What are some other incidences wherein God proved nothing was too hard for Him?

....

....

....

When has God done the impossible in your life or in the lives of your loved ones? What role did faith play in the situation(s)?

....

....

....

Why might your own thoughts or imagination keep you from seeing the possible?

....

....

....

Personal Peace Prayer

....

....

WHEN IN CRISIS MODE

Read Psalm 34:17–20; John 16:33

When was the last time you cried out to God for help? What did He do to remove your distress and trouble and help you bear up under it?

....

....

....

Although you may encounter evil, God will deliver you from it. How might that give you peace amid a crisis?

....

....

....

How does knowing Jesus has overcome the world and "deprived it of power to harm you and have conquered it for you" (John 16:33 AMPC) give you the calm you crave?

....

....

....

Personal Peace Prayer

....

....

WHEN FEELING UNLOVED

—— *Read Zephaniah 3:17; Psalm 136:26; Matthew 22:36–40* ——

How might knowing that God (who is love) will never betray, leave, or abandon you turn your thoughts of being unloved around?

....

....

....

Even when other things pass away, God's love will last forever. What eternal comfort does that give you?

....

....

....

How would not loving yourself make it harder for you to obey God's command to love Him and others?

....

....

....

Personal Peace Prayer

....

....

....

WHEN LADEN WITH SIN

Read Psalm 38; 103

Where do you go when your burdens become too heavy for you? To whom do you confess your missteps?

....

....

....

After God forgives your iniquities, how long is it before you forgive yourself? Why?

....

....

....

How does it feel knowing that God removes your sins "as far as the east is from the west" (Psalm 103:12 ESV)? Are you certain of this in your mind? Why or why not?

....

....

....

Personal Peace Prayer

....

....

WHEN OVERWHELMED

Read 2 Kings 6:8–23

In this story of far-seeing Elisha and his somewhat myopic servant, which role do you usually take on when the going gets tough?

....

....

....

Elisha saw things from God's perspective. How do *you* see things? How does that serve you?

....

....

....

In what ways does fear blind you? What words might you pray to God so that your eyes would be opened?

....

....

....

Personal Peace Prayer

....

....

....

WHEN GRIEVING

—— *Read Psalm 34:18; 147:3; Isaiah 53:4; John 14:1–4* ——

When have you felt the Lord very close to you even when you were brokenhearted? when you were still wounded by sorrow?

....

....

....

Jesus already carries your grief and sorrow. In what ways have you turned such burdens over to Him?

....

....

....

How does knowing God has a place prepared for all His children give you comfort?

....

....

....

Personal Peace Prayer

....

....

....

WHEN JOBLESS

*———— Read Genesis 28:15; Matthew 6:30–33; ————
Jeremiah 29:11; Philippians 4:6*

God, the One who keeps watch over you, has made some promises to you, promises He very much intends to keep. How might that soothe your spirits after you've lost your job?

....

....

....

What is Jesus' remedy for your being anxious about what the next days will bring? Which of those remedies have you taken to heart?

....

....

How does knowing God has a plan for all His seekers give you hope? What role can prayer and gratitude for God play right now?

....

....

....

Personal Peace Prayer

....

....

WHEN FACING DEATH

—— *Read Psalm 23; 48:14; Isaiah 41:10; 57:1–2; John 14:1–4* ——

What comfort do you find in Psalm 23? How does knowing God will be your guide forever give you comfort?

....

....

....

In His Word, God tells you repeatedly not to fear, that He will always uphold you no matter where, no matter when. What fears, if any, might you want to turn over to Him right now?

....

....

....

What peace do you get from knowing God has a room for you and Jesus has personally prepared it?

....

....

....

Personal Peace Prayer

....

....

WHEN NEEDING WISDOM

Read Proverbs 3:13–18; James 1:5; 3:17

Make a list of all the benefits you gain from seeking and finding wisdom. Which benefit would be the biggest blessing in your life?

....

....

....

When have you asked God for wisdom? What did He tell you? What did you do with it?

....

....

....

In what ways have you found God's wisdom to be peace-loving?

....

....

....

Personal Peace Prayer

....

....

....

WHEN DROWNING

—— *Read Jonah 2:2–7; Matthew 14:25–33; Ephesians 6:10–12* ——

When you are drowning in grief, heartache, or loss, what do your prayers to God look like?

....

....

....

What forms of relief did you find when spending time in prayer to God and in His presence? What happened when you took your eyes off Jesus during this time?

....

....

....

In what ways did God help you wrestle with the forces against you?

....

....

....

Personal Peace Prayer

....

....

....

WHEN ON THE RUN

Read 1 Kings 19

What fear(s) have ever prompted you to take a run?

....

....

....

How did God sustain you while you were in the wilderness? What did God tell you when you were calm enough to hear Him speak?

....

....

....

How did God help you find the peace and strength to stop running and take a stand?

....

....

....

Personal Peace Prayer

....

....

....

WHEN LEADING

—— *Read Proverbs 31:8–9; Mark 10:42–45; 1 Peter 5:2–4* ——

How do you find a way to speak for those who cannot speak for themselves?

....

....

....

In what ways do you serve others as you shepherd them? What kind of example did Jesus set for you? What kind of example are you setting for your flock?

....

....

....

Why do you serve—for what you will get out of it or because you are eager to serve the Lord?

....

....

....

Personal Peace Prayer

....

....

....

WHEN FOLLOWING

Read Deuteronomy 28:1–28; John 14:15

How, when, and where do you make yourself available for God to speak to you?

....

....

....

What does God promise you if you obey Him? What does God promise you if you disobey Him?

....

....

....

As you follow God, what are the two main commandments Jesus tells you to adhere to?

....

....

....

Personal Peace Prayer

....

....

....

WHEN SEEKING GOD

— *Read Deuteronomy 4:29; Matthew 6:33; 7:7–8; Hebrews 11:6* —

How are you to seek out or search after God? What does Jesus tell you to seek first? Why?

....

....

....

....

What is the great ASK formula? How does adhering to it give you peace?

....

....

....

In what ways do you think God rewards you for seeking Him?

....

....

....

Personal Peace Prayer

....

....

....

WHEN RESTLESS

Read Exodus 14:13; 1 Samuel 9:27; 12:7;
Job 37:14; Psalm 4:4; 46:10

Why did Moses tell his people to stand still? Why did Samuel tell Saul to stand still?

....

....

When was the last time you stood still and considered God's wonders? What was that experience like?

....

....

....

Why does God, speaking through the psalmist, urge you to "let be and be still, and know (recognize and understand) that I am God" (Psalm 46:10 AMPC)?

....

....

....

Personal Peace Prayer

....

....

WHEN TIRED OF PERSEVERING

— *Read 2 Samuel 21:1–14; Matthew 24:13; 1 Corinthians 9:24* —

What are you persevering at right now? What keeps you going?

....

....

....

What was Rizpah's supreme act of extreme perseverance? What do you think fueled her? What was the result of Rizpah's commitment to her cause? What lessons can you learn from her story?

....

....

....

What will happen to those who will endure to the end?

....

....

....

Personal Peace Prayer

....

....

....

WHEN TALKING TO OTHERS ABOUT GOD

Read Luke 12:9–12

In what ways, if any, does your anxiety show up when you are planning on talking to others about God?

....

....

....

When was the last time you shared with someone the Word of God? What was the result?

....

....

....

Who does Jesus say will help you when you can't find the words to share with others? When have you found that to be true for you?

....

....

....

Personal Peace Prayer

....

....

WHEN CORRECTING A WRONG

Read 1 Samuel 25

Who wronged David and his men? How were they wronged? How did David react?

....

....

....

Who tried to correct that wrong? What did she do?

....

....

....

What lessons about correcting your own wrongs can you learn from this story?

....

....

....

Personal Peace Prayer

....

....

....

WHEN SERVING GOD

Read John 14:12–14

How much confidence do you have in being able to do what God has called you to do?

....

....

....

What does Jesus say that gives you the confidence to serve Him?

....

....

....

What may you need to do in order to accomplish what God has called you to do?

....

....

....

Personal Peace Prayer

....

....

....

Keeping Your Peace When. . . — Day 42

WHEN IN A STRANGE PLACE

—————— *Read Genesis 28:10–19; Matthew 10:12–14; 28:20* ——————

When have you been somewhere strange and wondered if God was in that place? When you awoke, what made you realize God *was* in that place after all?

....

....

....

What does Jesus tell His disciples to do if a household is not worthy of their peace? Do you use that same tactic? Why or why not?

....

....

....

What makes you so sure that God will be with you no matter where you are or go?

....

....

....

Personal Peace Prayer

....

....

WHEN FACING ILLNESS

—— *Read Luke 12:4–9; 2 Corinthians 12:7; James 5:14–15* ——

What comfort do you find in the fact that whether you are feeling well or sick, God sees you and tenderly cares about you?

....

....

....

What thorns might God have given you? Why?

....

....

....

What remedies for illness does James offer? Which have you taken to heart?

....

....

....

Personal Peace Prayer

....

....

....

WHEN YOU NEED CONFIDENCE

—— *Read Jeremiah 17:7–8; Philippians 4:13; 2 Timothy 1:7* ——

Why "are those who trust in the LORD and have made the LORD their hope and confidence" (Jeremiah 17:7 NLT) blessed?

....

....

....

How does knowing you can do all things through Christ increase your level of confidence?

....

....

....

What words of God do you confidently say to yourself to boost your confidence?

....

....

....

Personal Peace Prayer

....

....

....

WHEN UNSURE OF YOUR CALLING

— *Read 2 Timothy 3:16–17; James 1:5; 2 Thessalonians 1:11–12* —

In what ways has God equipped you for your calling?

....

....

....

What wisdom have you sought from God regarding your calling? What has He shared with you?

....

....

....

What ability has God given you to accomplish what He has prompted you to do?

....

....

....

Personal Peace Prayer

....

....

....

WHEN BEREFT OF HOPE

— Read Genesis 21:1–2; Isaiah 40:31; Mark 9:23; Romans 15:13 —

God did (and will always do) as promised. How does that give you hope?

....

....

....

What happens when you wait on God and hope in Him?

....

....

....

Jesus says, "Everything is possible to the one who believes" (Mark 9:23 HCSB). How does that give you hope? Who is your source of hope?

....

....

....

Personal Peace Prayer

....

....

....

....

WHEN WORRIED ABOUT THE PAST

——— *Read Genesis 19:17, 26; Proverbs 4:25; Luke 9:62* ———

What happened to Lot's wife when she, despite the angels' warning, looked back at where she'd been?

....

....

....

Why is "no one who puts his hand to the plow and looks back. . .fit for the kingdom of God" (Luke 9:62 HCSB)?

....

....

....

Where are your eyes when you're worried about the past? Where should your eyes be? Why?

....

....

....

Personal Peace Prayer

....

....

....

WHEN CONCERNED
ABOUT YOUR TALENTS

—— *Read Matthew 25:14–30; Romans 12:6; 1 Peter 4:10* ——

Who fills you with talents? What are your talents? How do you use them to serve God and others?

....

....

....

What talents might you have buried? Why?

....

....

....

What are some talents God is bringing to your attention? When will you begin to use them?

....

....

....

Personal Peace Prayer

....

....

....

WHEN DETERMINED TO DO THE RIGHT THING

Read Luke 10:25–37

What does Jesus say are the two most important commandments?

....

....

....

How are you at doing for others? What have you done for others?

....

....

....

What can the proverb of the Good Samaritan teach you about doing the right thing?

....

....

....

Personal Peace Prayer

....

....

....

WHEN PLAGUED BY BITTERNESS

— Read Hebrews 12:14–15; Matthew 18:21–22; Ephesians 4:31–32 —

Is your heart bitter? If so, how does that keep you from finding peace? How might your bitterness lead you to seek God's love and forgiveness?

....

....

....

....

Jesus says you need to forgive others to be forgiven by God. How many times are you to do so? What things are there, if any, that you need to forgive yourself for?

....

....

....

....

....

Personal Peace Prayer

....

....

....

....

WHEN YOU'RE RAISING KIDS

—— *Read Proverbs 22:6; 29:17; Isaiah 54:13; Matthew 18:1–3* ——

Many have heard that if you put your kids on the right path, they'll stick to it as they grow older. But rarely is one reminded that if you correct your kids, you'll have peace of mind. How is that working in your life?

....

....

God tells His people that the children He teaches will "enjoy great peace" (Isaiah 54:13 NLT). When have you witnessed that? What does that tell you about who your God is?

....

....

....

You can not only teach your children but learn from them. In what ways has a child shown you how to become like him or her so that you can enter the kingdom of heaven?

....

....

....

Personal Peace Prayer

....

....

WHEN TRAVELING

—— *Read Deuteronomy 31:8; Psalm 121:7–8; 139:9–10* ——

What peace do you find in knowing God is already in the place you have determined to go, checking things out before you had any idea you'd be traveling?

....

....

....

God has His eye on you, watching over you as you come and go. How will you keep your eye on Him as you come and go?

....

....

....

Where have you gone and realized God was right there with you, holding your hand, guiding you, supporting you?

....

....

....

Personal Peace Prayer

....

....

WHEN THE WORLD SEEMS TO BE FALLING APART

— *Read Jeremiah 29:11–13; Isaiah 41:10–13; 2 Thessalonians 3:16* —

How does knowing God has a plan for you help you when your world seems to be falling apart?

....

....

....

No matter what is happening in your life, God has a firm grip on you. In what ways do you make sure you have a firm grip on Him?

....

....

....

What route is open to you when you need peace from the Prince of Peace? How often do you take that route?

....

....

....

Personal Peace Prayer

....

....

WHEN YOU'RE TAKING
A LEAP OF FAITH

Read Psalm 9:10; Philippians 1:6; Hebrews 12:1–3

When was the last time you took a leap of faith?

....

....

....

Before you took even one step, what was your level of trust in the One who created the entire universe—including you? How did that help you keep your calm?

....

....

....

How can you be assured that you'll have the resources to accomplish your purpose and be successful in your endeavor?

....

....

....

Personal Peace Prayer

....

....

WHEN THE DARKNESS SEEMS OVERWHELMING

—— *Read Deuteronomy 31:8; Psalm 40:1–3; Romans 8:38–39* ——

How does knowing God is with you and will never leave you give you the courage to face the darkness?

....

....

....

God promises to turn to you, draw you up out of the pit, set your feet upon a rock, ensure you can walk, and put a new song in your mouth. But what do you need to do first?

....

....

....

What peace do you find knowing the Lord of Light and Love is and always will be with you, no matter what, no matter where you are?

....

....

Personal Peace Prayer

....

....

WHEN FEELING ALONE

—— *Read Deuteronomy 31:6, 8; Psalm 23:1; 27:10; John 14:18* ——

You cannot outrun, outpace, outthink, or outlive the Lord who goes before you, comes behind you, and is by your side. So, what makes you think you are or ever will be alone?

....

....

....

If you feel alone from everyone—including God—who has moved?

....

....

....

How does it feel knowing that no matter who has deserted you in the past or present, God is the one Parent who will always take you in, give you room, care for you?

....

....

....

Personal Peace Prayer

....

....

WHEN FEELING UNTETHERED

—— *Read Psalm 34:18; 121:1–2; Zephaniah 3:17; Colossians 3:2* ——

How do you reconcile feeling disconnected from God when all you have to do is lift your eyes and see that He is near the brokenhearted and ready to rescue those crushed in spirit?

....

....

....

God is not only with you, acting as your anchor, but He's rejoicing over you, calming you with His love, and shouting over you with joy. Listen. What is He saying to you today?

....

....

....

If you're feeling untethered, what might happen if you set your mind, your focus, and your eyes on the higher things rather than those things that may be putting you off-kilter?

....

....

Personal Peace Prayer

....

....

WHEN MONEY IS TIGHT

—— *Read Psalm 94:19; Matthew 6:34; Philippians 4:6, 19* ——

When you're anxious about finances or anything else for that matter, where do you go for comfort and hope? Where can you go?

....

....

....

What advice does Jesus give you about worrying today? In what ways can or do you follow that advice?

....

....

....

What must you do to have your needs met? Are you doing so? Why or why not?

....

....

....

Personal Peace Prayer

....

....

....

WHEN PLANS GO AWRY

—— *Read Psalm 34:1–7; Proverbs 3:5–8; Habakkuk 3:17–19* ——

Some plans succeed. Some go awry. How would you and your world shift—within and without—if you praised the Lord either way?

....

....

....

How might trusting in God and His wisdom instead of you and your wisdom bring you peace during easy and hard times?

....

....

....

What does God do no matter how your plans go?

....

....

....

Personal Peace Prayer

....

....

....

WHEN YOU'RE A WORK STILL IN PROGRESS

Read Psalm 16:8; Proverbs 12:25; Hebrews 13:6

What can you do to make sure you're not shaken up while you, like all great works, are in progress?

....

....

....

What good words from God encourage you the most? Which have you memorized?

....

....

....

What will it take for you to say with confidence, "God is with me, helping me, protecting me, loving me; so, I have no fear—only hope and peace in Him"?

....

....

Personal Peace Prayer

....

....

DAILY BIBLE STUDY MADE SIMPLE WITH THEMED READING PLANS!

Do you want to spend time in God's Word, but aren't sure where to start? *My Bible Study Journal* can help!

These elegant journals feature six 30-day Bible reading plans that will encourage you to delve deeper into God's Word.

Each entry includes the scripture reference for the day's Bible reading and journaling prompts with ample lined space that will encourage you to reflect, applying God's Word to your own life and heart.

My Bible Study Journals are perfect for your own personal quiet time or small group study!

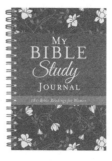

Spiral Bound / 978-1-68322-415-0 / $7.99

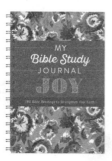

Spiral Bound / 978-1-64352-444-3 / $9.99